FORMULA ONE
RACE CARS

by Janet Piehl

Jan Lahtonen, consultant and safety engineer, auto mechanic, and lifelong Formula One enthusiast

Lerner Publications Company • Minneapolis

For Sara Lovas

Cover photo: Australian Mark Webber, of the Williams-BMW team, leads the pack at the 2005 Grand Prix of Monaco. Webber would go on to finish third in the race. Finn Kimi Raikkonen of the McLaren Mercedes Team won the race. Webber's teammate, German Nick Heidfeld, finished second.

Lerner Publications Company
A division of Lerner Publishing Group
241 First Avenue North
Minneapolis, MN 55401 U.S.A.

Website address: www.lernerbooks.com

Library of Congress Cataloging-in-Publication Data

Piehl, Janet.
      Formula one race cars / by Janet Piehl.
          p.   cm. — (Motor Mania)
      Includes bibliographical references and index.
      ISBN-13: 978–0–8225–5929–0 (lib. bdg. : alk. paper)
      ISBN-10: 0–8225–5929–3 (lib. bdg. : alk. paper)
      1. Formula One automobiles—Juvenile literature.
   2. Automobile racing—Juvenile literature. I. Title.
   II. Series: Motor Mania (Minneapolis, Minn.)
   TL236.P5272 2007
   629.228—dc22   2005020822

Manufactured in the United States of America
1 2 3 4 5 6 – DP – 12 11 10 09 08 07

Contents

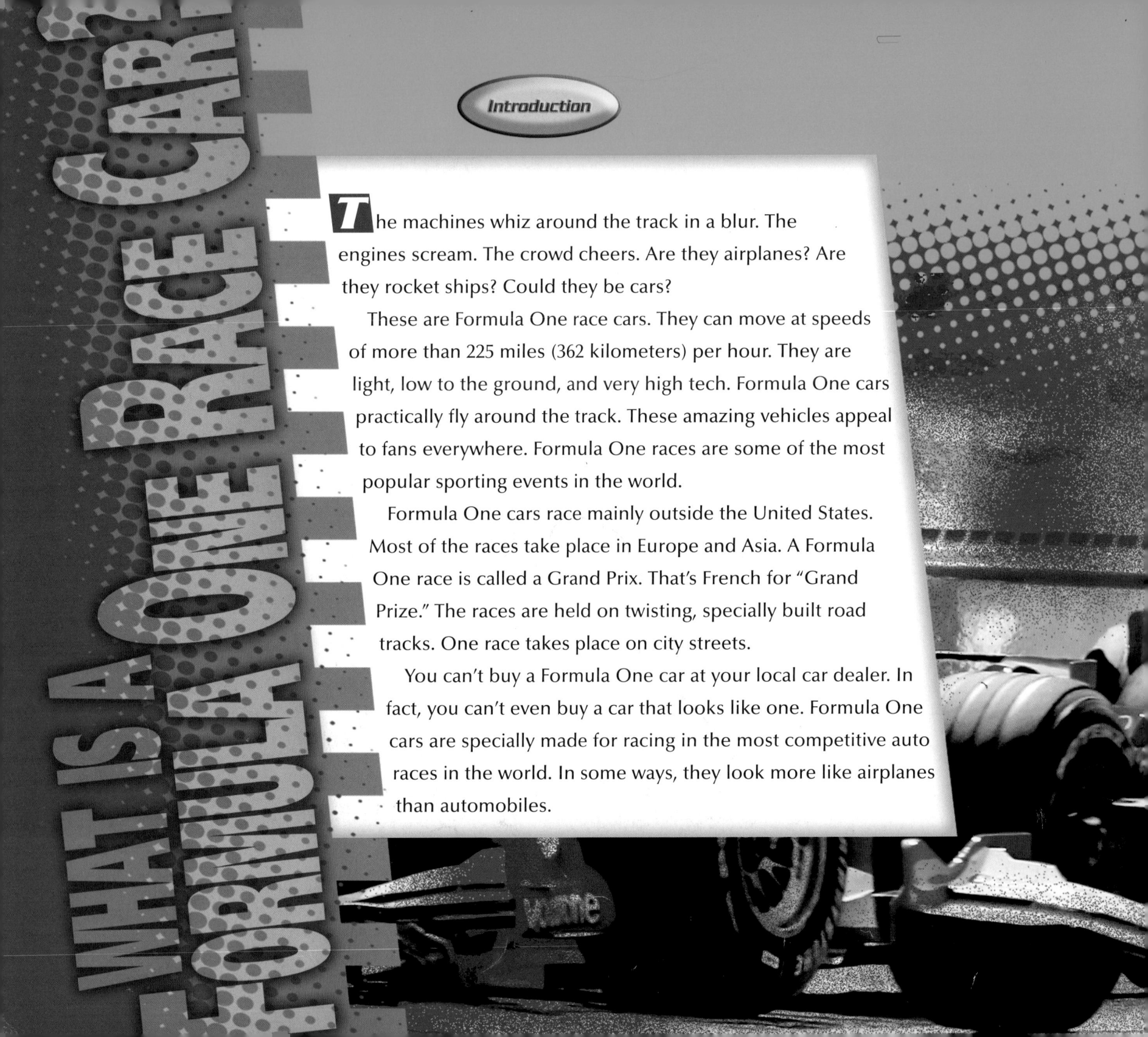

Introduction

*T*he machines whiz around the track in a blur. The engines scream. The crowd cheers. Are they airplanes? Are they rocket ships? Could they be cars?

These are Formula One race cars. They can move at speeds of more than 225 miles (362 kilometers) per hour. They are light, low to the ground, and very high tech. Formula One cars practically fly around the track. These amazing vehicles appeal to fans everywhere. Formula One races are some of the most popular sporting events in the world.

Formula One cars race mainly outside the United States. Most of the races take place in Europe and Asia. A Formula One race is called a Grand Prix. That's French for "Grand Prize." The races are held on twisting, specially built road tracks. One race takes place on city streets.

You can't buy a Formula One car at your local car dealer. In fact, you can't even buy a car that looks like one. Formula One cars are specially made for racing in the most competitive auto races in the world. In some ways, they look more like airplanes than automobiles.

A pack of Formula One race cars battle for position at the start of a Grand Prix race in Kuala Lumpur, Malaysia. Formula One racing is one of the world's most popular sports, with Grand Prix races held on five continents.

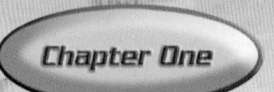

Chapter One

HISTORY OF FORMULA ONE RACE CARS

During a Formula One race, computers keep track of nearly every part of the car, including the brakes, engine, and traction control.

To understand the history of Formula One cars, it helps to know what the newest Formula One cars look like. Formula One cars are called open-wheel race cars. Open-wheel cars have no fenders over their wheels. Drivers sit in open cockpits. They have no roofs over their heads. Formula One cars look a lot like Indy cars—open-wheel cars that race in the Indianapolis 500 and in other races that take place mostly in the United States.

Each Formula One car has a narrow chassis. The chassis is the basic frame of the car. The engine and all the other parts are attached to the chassis. The suspension connects the wheels to the chassis.

Modern Formula One cars have wings in front and on the back. The wings work in the opposite way of aircraft wings. They create downforce. As the car moves, air goes over the wings and pushes the car down. Downforce keeps the car from tipping over or sliding off the track. It allows the cars to zip around curves at high speeds.

Formula One cars have smooth bodywork on the outside. The shape of the cars makes them aerodynamic. Air flows easily over them and slows them down as little as possible.

With their slick looks, Formula One cars look like they're from the future. But their history goes all the way back to some of the first cars.

During a race, crews and engineers working at the track send data about how this Formula One car is running to the factory where the car was built. Factory engineers can go over the data and send back instructions for how to adjust the car to make it faster.

The Starting Grid

If it moves, people will race it. The first cars were invented in the late 1800s, and the first races came soon after. The roots of Formula One racing go back to these early events. Drivers held the first auto races in both Europe and the United States in 1894. In 1906, the Automobile Club of France organized the first Grand Prix. Like modern race cars, the Grand Prix cars were built just for racing. Like modern cars, they had open wheels and open cockpits. But these first cars were large and boxy. Still, they could travel at about 100 miles (160 km) per hour. But the machines tended to break down a lot. So a mechanic often

In the early 1900s, race cars were fast but not safe. When they crashed, drivers had almost no protection from injury. Many accidents were deadly.

rode along to help with emergency repairs.

Back then, cars raced mostly on public roads that were closed off for the day. The races were dangerous for both drivers and fans. The unreliable, unsafe cars sometimes spun out of control and into the onlooking crowds. Drivers and fans were killed. Some countries discouraged Grand Prix races because they were so deadly. But fans still wanted the thrill of watching fast cars. So people built tracks just for racing. Walls separated the fans from the tracks. This took some of the danger out of the sport.

Grand Prix races continued in Europe during the first half of the 1900s. No races were held during World War I (1914–1918) and World War II (1939–1945). In 1948, an organization known as the Fédération Internationale de l'Automobile (International Federation of the Automobile, or FIA) created a set of rules for racing.

German Engineering

Some of the fastest Grand Prix cars ever made were built in Germany in the 1930s. German leader Adolf Hitler wanted to show the world that Germans could build the fastest cars. So he ordered two companies, Mercedes and Auto Union, to build the best Grand Prix racing cars possible. German cars like this Auto Union (*right*) went on to win every Grand Prix race in the world from 1935 to 1939.

The name "Formula One" refers to the formula, or set of rules, that determines how the race cars are designed and built. The formula helped to even out the competition among cars.

The first Formula One race was held in 1948 in Pau, France. The Formula One World Championship began in 1950. It was a series of seven races—six in Europe and one in the United

Juan Manuel Fangio *(left)* of Argentina roars past the wreckage of his competitors on the way to another win in 1957. Fangio's record of five Formula One World Championships remained unmatched until the 2000s.

States. Drivers won points based on how well they finished in each race. A race's winner received the most points. The second-place finisher received the second-most points and so on. The driver who won the most points during the series earned the title of World Champion.

During the 1950s, Formula One cars raced on both roads and road tracks. The cars were low to the ground. They were shaped like cigars. The engine was in the front of the car, and the driver sat up straight in the cock-

pit. Only one person could sit in the cockpit. The mechanic had long been left behind.

Formula One racing quickly caught on. Its audience soon grew beyond Europe and the United States. In 1953, a Grand Prix was held for the first time in the South American country of Argentina. In 1958, the racing series went to North Africa for a Grand Prix in Morocco. Italian and Argentine drivers led the way. Juan Manuel Fangio of Argentina won five World Championships in the 1950s.

How an Internal Combustion Engine Works

Formula One race car engines are some of the most high-tech machines ever built. But they still create power through internal combustion, just like normal cars. Like road cars, Formula One engines run on fuel use a "four stroke" cycle (*right*). This process burns a mixture of air and fuel that is similar to the gasoline road cars use. They power the car. Over the years, Formula One engines have changed in many ways. They have had as few as six cylinders and as many as twelve.

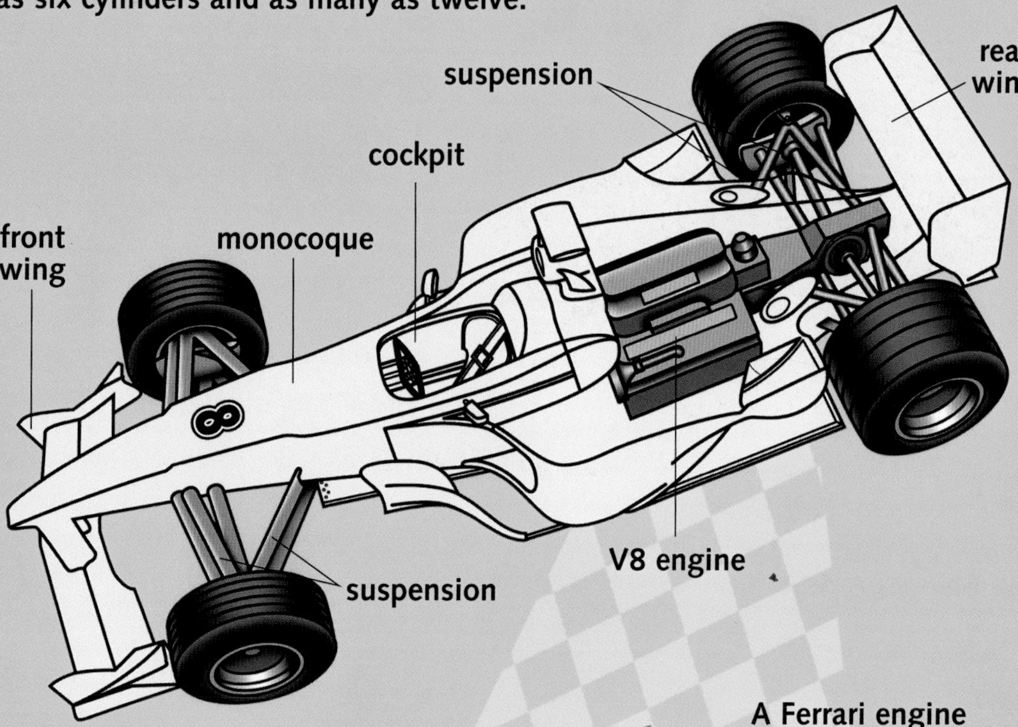

suspension

rear wing

cockpit

front wing

monocoque

suspension

V8 engine

A Ferrari engine

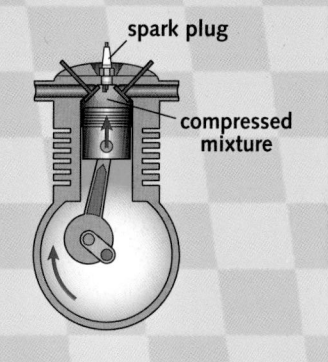

intake valve

fuel-air mixture

cylinder

piston

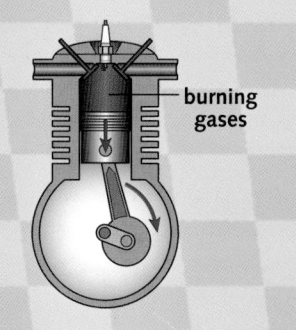

spark plug

compressed mixture

burning gases

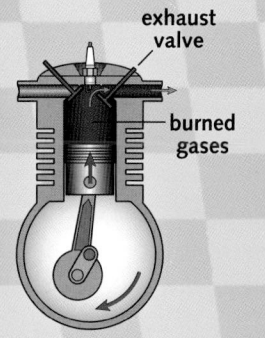

exhaust valve

burned gases

In 1958, the FIA decided to honor not only drivers but the teams, or constructors, who built and took care of the cars. So it began awarding the World Constructors' Championship. Drivers were no longer the only ones who gained fame. The drivers were supported by an army of engineers, mechanics, and builders. The title went to the team whose two drivers scored the most points in a season. The World Constructors' Championship is still awarded.

Technical Changes

Each season, the cars change. Changes that help cars win races tend to become permanent. In the late 1950s, teams began making cars with engines in the rear or mid-section, behind the driver. Cars with rear engines proved to be faster than front-engine cars. By then, better technology had produced newer, smaller engines that could fit in the rear. Without a bulky engine in front, a car could have a flatter, smoother front section. This made the car more aerodynamic. Putting the engine in the rear also made the car less front-heavy. It gave the racer better balance. This change made the car easier to handle, especially around corners.

Going in Different Directions

When the first racetracks were built in the early 1900s, Europeans designed their tracks to go in a clockwise direction. But Americans made their racetracks go in a counterclockwise direction. The Americans also designed their track with the spectator in mind. They built short, round tracks that allowed fans to watch the entire race from a grandstand. This trend has lived on with American stock car racing and Indy car racing. Europeans, however, preferred road course racing. Road courses, like those in Formula One, are several miles long and have many curves. The fans, however, can only see a section of the race at any one time.

British two-time World Champion Jim Clark behind the wheel of a rear-engine Lotus before a 1965 race. One of Formula One's greatest drivers, he was killed in a mysterious accident in a non-Formula One race in 1968.

British driver Stirling Moss was the first to win a race in a car with a rear engine. He won the 1958 Argentine Grand Prix in a rear-engined Cooper. Soon cars with rear engines started winning more and more races. By the early 1960s, all Formula One cars had engines in the rear.

The 1960s brought more big changes to the design of Formula One cars. Until then, each racer had a chassis that was shaped like a ladder. Two long tubes ran down either side of the bottom of the car. Shorter tubes going across the car connected the long tubes. The body, or main part of the car, was mounted on the chassis.

But in 1962, an exciting new design came out—the Lotus 25. It had a monocoque construction. The chassis was a single tube-shaped shell—the monocoque. The other parts of the car were attached to it. A monocoque looked a lot like a bathtub, with a hole cut out for the cockpit.

The new design was made of lightweight aluminum. It weighed far less than the old style of chassis. The aluminum was very strong too. It made the new cars safer in accidents. Because of the new design, the driver no longer sat up straight. He would practically lie down in the cockpit. Overall, the car was much

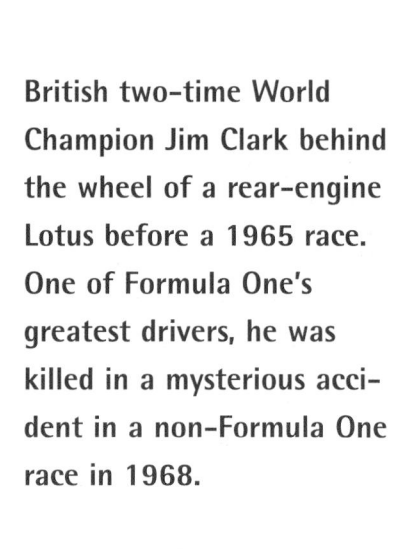

A DANGEROUS SPORT

Early Formula One cars had few safety features. Other than seatbelts and helmets, drivers had little protection from crashes. As a result, many drivers were killed in wrecks during the early decades of the sport.

Three-time World Champion Jackie Stewart of Britain in his winged Matra Ford car in 1969 *(below)*. The addition of wings allowed the cars to reach even higher speeds than before.

American Mario Andretti in his Lotus in 1978 *(right)*, the year he won the World Championship. By the late 1970s, Formula One cars had become more streamlined than ever before. The pods on the sides of the car held radiators—devices that cool the engine.

lower and shorter, making it more aerodynamic.

Another aerodynamic improvement came in 1968. Cars began to feature wings on the front and back. The cars' wings are shaped a lot like upside-down airplane wings. Teams experimented with wings of different shapes, sizes, and positions on cars. The wings made the cars faster and more stable in turns. But they also could cause accidents. The wrong amount of downforce could make a car hard to steer. And wings sometimes broke off during races. So the FIA created rules to limit the size and placement of wings.

British drivers were the kings of the track during the 1960s. They won several World Championships in the 1960s and early 1970s. Racers Graham Hill, Jackie Stewart, and Jim Clark won the championship seven times among them.

By the late 1970s, Formula One teams had begun working with another way to create downforce—ground effects. Teams sculpted the underside of their cars in a special way. Air flowed beneath the car, and the ground effects created a suction effect. The changes made enough downforce to practically glue the car to the track. The racers could go around corners at higher speeds than ever. Lotus introduced Formula One cars with ground effects in the late 1970s. American Mario Andretti won the World Championship in 1978 driving cars with ground effects for Lotus.

But like wings, ground effects could be tricky and dangerous. Cars with ground effects could go at dangerously high speeds. And the cars were sometimes hard to steer. This made for a risky mix. Ground effects were thought to be so risky that they were banned from Formula One in 1983.

Fast Competition and Better Safety

As the 1980s went on, Formula One cars got lighter and more aerodynamic. They had also become safer. Fewer and fewer drivers were killed. Meanwhile, the competition became fiercer. Drivers such as Alain Prost, Ayrton Senna, Nelson Piquet, and Nigel Mansell chased one another to victory. Races expanded to more and more countries. New Grand Prix races were held in Australia in 1985 and Japan in 1987.

Only two women drivers have competed in Formula One racing. Maria Theresa de Filippis raced in the 1950s. Lella Lombardi (left) raced in the 1970s.

Ayrton Senna's fatal crash at the San Marino Grand Prix in 1994 shocked the racing world and led to many changes to increase driver safety. Senna's injuries were caused not by the impact of the car but by a piece of the car, which broke off and struck him.

In 1994, three-time World Champion Ayrton Senna was looking forward to another fast season. He was in the lead at the San Marino Grand Prix in Italy when his car slammed into a wall. He later died from his injuries. Something may have gone wrong with his car, but no one knows exactly why he crashed.

Senna's death and several other serious accidents forced the FIA to create tougher safety rules. The organization limited the speed and power of the cars. Teams came up with newer, safer cockpit designs. The new cockpits offered drivers better protection, especially around the driver's head.

Officials added safety features to tracks too. Gravel traps were installed on the edges of some parts of tracks. If a car runs off the track, the gravel will slow it down. Tires block some walls along tracks. The tires work as cushions. They make crashes with walls less destructive.

The year of Senna's death, Michael Schumacher won his first World Championship. The skillful German took the title again in 1995. Five years later, he began a run of success never before seen in Formula One.

The car of Christian Klien of the Red Bull team tumbles during a crash on the first lap of the 2005 Hungarian Grand Prix in Budapest, Hungary. The first lap is usually the most dangerous lap of the race. At this stage, all of the cars are crammed together on the track and fighting for position.

World Champion Michael Schumacher during his time with the Benetton team in the early 1990s. After winning two titles with Benetton, the German ace moved on to Ferrari and won five more titles.

The Age of Schumacher and Beyond

Schumacher won the World Championship in 2000. He followed this up by winning the next four titles in a row. By 2004, Schumacher had seven World Championships to his credit. He holds the records for the most total wins, most wins in a season, most points in a season, and several other achievements. By the numbers, he is the best Formula One driver ever.

But Schumacher's reign could not last forever. In 2005, he was finally overtaken by Fernando Alonso. The 24-year-old Spaniard became the youngest Formula One World Champion ever, and his Renault team won the World Constructors' Championship. Another rising star, Kimi Räikkönen of Finland, finished second. Schumacher came in third.

Other changes have come to Formula One in recent years. New Grand Prix races have been added to the schedule. In 2005, the first Grand Prix was held on a brand-new course in Turkey. The year before, China and the Middle Eastern country of Bahrain also hosted their first Grand Prix races.

The FIA rule changes continue to keep teams on their toes. For 2006, FIA changed the rule for engines. Cars began running on new V8 engines instead of the V10s that were used in years past. The new

It Runs in the Family

The love of racing seems to be a family trait. Graham Hill and his son Damon were both Formula One World Champions. Jacques Villeneuve took after his father, Gilles, by racing in Formula One. Three members of the Fittipaldi family were Formula One drivers—Wilson, Christian, and two-time World Champion Emerson. Michael Schumacher's brother Ralf is also a Formula One competitor.

engines are expected to be less expensive to build and maintain. The new, less powerful engines will also make the cars a little slower—and safer—for drivers.

These yearly changes bring new challenges for drivers and teams. The teams must adapt and find ways to get the most out of their cars. And this is what Formula One is all about. It's about who can build the fastest, smartest car and who can drive it most skillfully. It's about the triumph of human and machine, working together to push the boundaries of technology.

A car from the McLaren-Mercedes team roars around a turn at the Grand Prix of Monaco. Each year, the FIA adjusts the rules for Formula One, bringing new challenges to the competition.

19

FORMULA ONE CULTURE

A Grand Prix has been compared to a circus coming to town. Tons of equipment—including the cars—must be transported to the race site. The cars and the track must be prepared. Television and newspaper reporters swarm the track. The excitement appeals to everyone from the drivers to the spectators. Formula One is about danger, drama, and sheer fun. What goes into the Formula One circus?

Revving Up for the Season

Running just one Formula One team involves many people and millions of dollars. Working for a team is a huge, exciting, and demanding job. Every year, the FIA releases a new set of rules, or formula. Teams work from

the formula to build the cars from the ground up.

Formula One cars are built and run by teams made up of car engineers, builders, mechanics, and drivers. Teams that compete in Formula One include Ferrari, BAR-Honda, Renault, McLaren-Mercedes, Toyota, and Red Bull. Many teams are run by big car companies. Team members come from all over the world, but the teams are based in one or two countries. For example, Ferrari is based in Italy. McLaren-Mercedes is British and German.

Over the fall and winter, engineers and mechanics work to build the fastest, safest car possible. They test different parts of the car and how they work together. Once the car is

A crowd of Spanish Formula One fans cheer for their countryman and favorite driver, Fernando Alonso. National pride is a big part of Formula One. Fans live and die for the success and failures of racers from their countries.

21

The beautiful track in Bahrain in the Middle East held its first Formula One race in 2004.

Each year, teams unveil their new cars and engines. Here Fernando Alonso *(left)* and Giancarlo Fisichella of Renault present the team's new engine.

built, the team tests it on a track. Test drivers check the cars to see what improvements need to be made. The car may go back to the factory for changes and more testing. Finally, the car is ready to race.

In the meantime, drivers get in shape for the season. They exercise and eat healthy food. They strengthen their arms, neck, back, and stomach. The races are exhausting, and the drivers must remain physically strong and mentally alert. Each team usually has two drivers.

The Track

Grand Prix races are held in Europe, Asia, Australia, South America, North America, and the Middle East. Most of them take place on specially built tracks. One race, the Monaco Grand Prix, is run on the city's streets. The streets are blocked off to regular traffic as the race winds through the city. Unlike most American racetracks, Formula One racetracks are not ovals. Instead, they may twist and turn. Like regular roads, they have long straight sections, bends, slopes, and tight curves.

Following the Line

Formula One courses are very different from the oval tracks of NASCAR and the Indy Racing League. The wide mix of turns, curves, and dips require a lot of driving skill. This is why Formula One drivers are known as the best in the world. The key to fast driving is to follow the "line"– the fastest route around the course. Drivers must slow down and turn the wheels as little as possible at each turn.

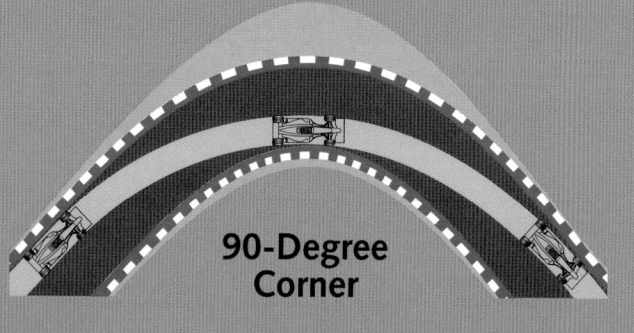

90-Degree Corner

A 90-degree turn is an L-shaped turn. The fastest way to pass through this turn is to start at the outside of the track. The driver then makes as wide a turn as possible, moving to the inside in the middle of the turn and coming to the outside at the finish.

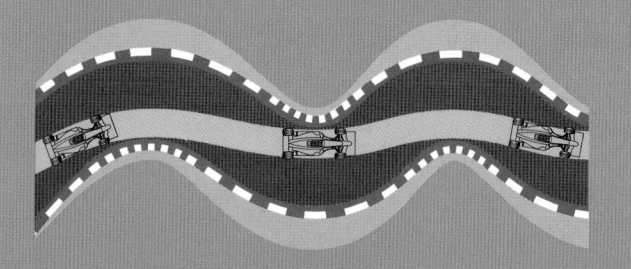

"S" Bend or Chicane

A chicane or S-bend is often found in the middle of a long, straight part of the course. A chicane forces the driver to slow down. The fastest way to slip through these curves is by going as straight as possible.

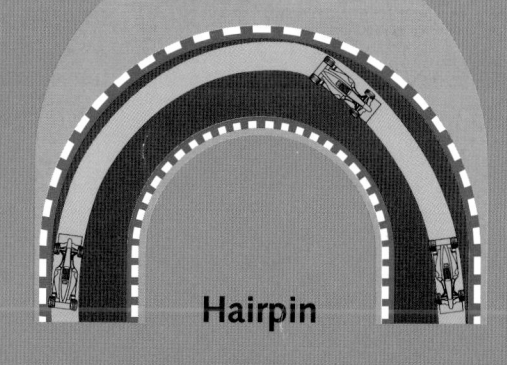

Hairpin

A hairpin turn gets its name from its shape–it looks like a long, U-shaped hairpin. Most come at the end of a long straight. The trick to hairpins is for the driver to judge how much to slow down to complete the turn.

Double-Apex Corner

A double-apex corner is two 90-degree turns connected by a short straight. The key to speeding through these is to keep a steady line all the way through.

Qualifying for the Race

The weekend of a Grand Prix starts on Thursday morning, when the drivers and teams arrive at the track. By Friday the team has set up the car, and the driver has time to test the car on the track. The driver talks to the team about the best settings for the car in the race. For example, the brakes, wings, or engine might need to be adjusted according to the track and even the weather. The tiniest changes can give a car an extra edge during the race. It could mean the difference between winning and finishing far behind the leader.

Formula for Success

Formula One racing is the top racing league in the world. How do drivers reach this level? Many future Formula One drivers start out racing karts as kids. Karts are small, light race cars. Some drivers attend special driving schools. They develop their skills in lower-level open-wheel racing series, such as GP2, Formula Ford, and Formula BMW. Many drivers compete in a lower-level circuit known as Formula Three. Only the very best drivers make the jump to Formula One.

Mechanics and engineers are the heroes of any racing team. They work long hours to build and maintain cars at their peak. Here a team of mechanics and engineers tests and sets up Michael Schumacher's Ferrari.

The drivers and teams also discuss the race strategy. Drivers study past races at each track. They try to find the fastest way around the course. They look for the best spot to hit the brakes before a turn. Drivers need to know the right place to come out of the turn going as fast as possible. They look for straight paths through big curves that don't force them to slow down very much. Teams also need to choose the right tires. Softer or harder tires will grip the track differently in different weather.

Practice sessions take place on both Friday and Saturday. By Saturday afternoon, it's time for the qualifying session. For 2006, Formula One introduced a new qualifying system in which drivers compete in three "knockout" rounds. The fastest cars in each round move on to the next round. For the final round, the top ten cars try for the fastest lap time.

The winner gets to start the race in pole position. The pole is the first position in the starting grid on the inside of the front row. Cars line up two-by-two in the starting grid.

Safety

Before even starting the race, the drivers take steps to avoid injury. Accidents can start fires, so drivers wear fireproof clothing. This includes long underwear, coveralls, gloves, and shoes. They even wear special fireproof face masks. Drivers wear strong helmets too.

Modern cars are much safer compared to the early days of Formula

The U-shaped markings in the starting grid show the starting position of each car.

Ralf Schumacher in his fireproof suit.

The HANS system attaches to the driver's helmet. It keeps the driver's head from snapping around violently during a crash.

One. Back then, drivers were frequently killed during races. For example, between 1960 and 1969, 27 drivers lost their lives. During the 1980s, 7 drivers were killed while racing. But no driver has been killed in a Formula One race since 1994.

One reason for the series' good safety record in recent years is the cars' many safety devices. Drivers are strapped into the cockpit with strong harnesses. This keeps them from flying out of the car in a wreck. Each Formula One car has a roll bar behind the driver's head. The roll bar protects the driver from being crushed in a rollover. Other safety features include removable steering wheels. Popping off the steering wheel allows the driver to escape the car quickly after a crash.

One of the newest Formula One safety features is the Head and Neck Support (HANS) system. It is a special collar and set of straps that hold up a driver's head in a collision. The collar and straps are connected to the car's safety harnesses and the driver's helmet. The system keeps the driver's head from whipping violently when the car comes to a sudden stop.

The cars themselves are built to protect the drivers from injury. Modern monocoques are made of carbon fiber, making them light yet strong. It protects most of a driver's body in a crash. And cars have rear lights so that other competitors can see them in the rain. Formula One races take place rain or shine, unless the conditions become too hazardous.

The Race

Races are held on Sunday afternoons. About 20 drivers qualify for each race. Before the competition begins, cars line up in the starting grid. An excited crowd fills the stands around the track. The team's planning and preparation are about to pay off. The red lights turn off and the cars take off.

Engines scream and the crowd cheers as another Spanish Grand Prix begins.

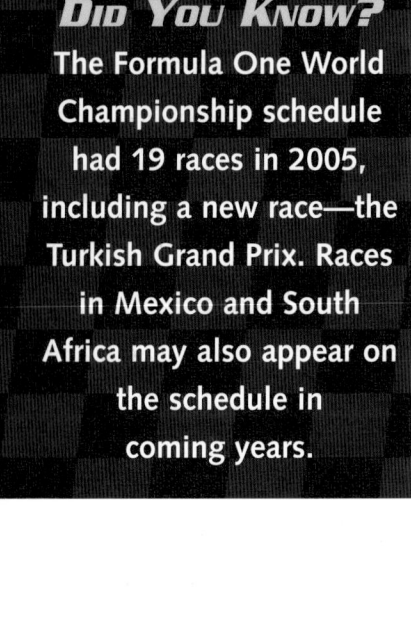

Each race is about 180 miles (290 km) long. The race must stop after two hours. Most races last only an hour and a half. The cars travel at average speeds of more than 100 miles (160 km) per hour. In straight parts of the track, cars can go more than 225 (362 km) miles per hour.

The cars roar around and around the track. Each driver tries to follow the strategy that he and his team have planned. They speed up and slow down in just the right places. Drivers watch the other cars carefully, looking out for accidents and figuring out ways to get ahead. An important move is overtaking, or passing. For example, a driver may pass another car by sneaking to the inside of the track on a curve.

Flags

Grand Prix officials use flags to communicate with drivers during the race. Each color has a different meaning.

Green: **Go. The race is on. Or, all clear. The danger has passed.**

Yellow: **Caution. Slow down.**

Red: **Danger. The race is stopped. This may be because of an accident or dangerous track conditions.**

Blue: **Warns a driver that he is about to be overtaken**

Yellow and red: **Slippery track**

Black and orange: **Tells a driver he has a mechanical problem and must return to the pit**

Half black, half white: **Warns a driver that he is showing unsportsmanlike behavior**

Black: **Tells a driver to return to the pit and that he may be eliminated from the race**

White: **Slow car on the track or one lap left in the race**

Checkered: **End of the race**

Drafting is another overtaking technique. The trailing car follows close behind the one in front of it. Because the first car blocks the wind, it cuts down the drag, or air resistance, of the second car. At just the right moment, the second car uses the advantage to zip past the first.

The teams make sure to fill up their cars' tanks with the proper amount of fuel. Of course, more fuel allows the car to travel farther without a fill-up. But carrying more fuel also adds weight and reduces speed. On the other hand, less fuel makes a car lighter and faster. But then the car risks running out of fuel before reaching the finish line. The trick is to carry just the right amount.

To refuel during the race, cars use pit stops. Pit stops can also be used to make repairs or adjustments to the car, if necessary. The pit is an area next to the track. During a pit stop, the driver pulls into the pit lane, slows down, and stops in the team's pit area. The team's pit crew leaps into action. The idea is to get the car back on the track as fast as possible. Every member of the pit crew has a special job to do. For example, one person handles the fuel container. Another adjusts the car's wings, if needed, and so on.

Pit crews spend thousands of hours practicing pit stops. They must work together perfectly to make the pit stop as fast as possible. Most last between six and twelve seconds.

F1 ON TV
In the United States, the Speed Channel cable network has complete coverage of Formula One races. Visit http://speedtv.com for listings.

The crew springs into action during a pit stop at the Spanish Grand Prix.

Michael Schumacher raises a fist to celebrate another Formula One victory.

The Finish

After almost two hours of intense mental and physical competition, the race comes to the finish line. Usually, a few drivers have dropped out because of mechanical problems or accidents. The remaining drivers try to overtake one more car or break a personal record. They zoom across the finish line. The checkered flag comes out, and one lucky—and skilled—driver wins.

All of this excitement pays off for the winner. He gets points toward the World Championship. He also wins money. These prize winnings come on top of each drivers' multimillion-dollar salary. For example, seven-time World Champion Schumacher earns a big salary from Ferrari. Many businesses

pay him big bucks to advertise their products. Schumacher made at least $80 million in 2004.

Fans

With races on five continents and drivers from all over the world, Formula One is one of the world's most popular sports. An estimated 300 million fans follow the racing series. At least 6,000 journalists report on the World Championship.

Each country has its heroes, and each fan has favorite cars and drivers. Italians adore Ferrari. Brazilians still mourn the death of Ayrton Senna. And Germans rally around Michael Schumacher. There's something for everyone in Formula One—high technology, speed, danger, suspense, glamour, tragedy, and glory.

After every race, the top three finishers stand at the podium and receive their trophies. In a longstanding tradition, the drivers then celebrate by dousing each other with champagne.

Another Formula One tradition allows fans to storm the track to celebrate after a race.

Formula One Grand Prix Courses

Formula One holds races all over the world, on five different continents. Each course is completely unique, with its own special shape and challenges for the driver. Here is a map of nineteen courses being used by Formula One in the 2000s.

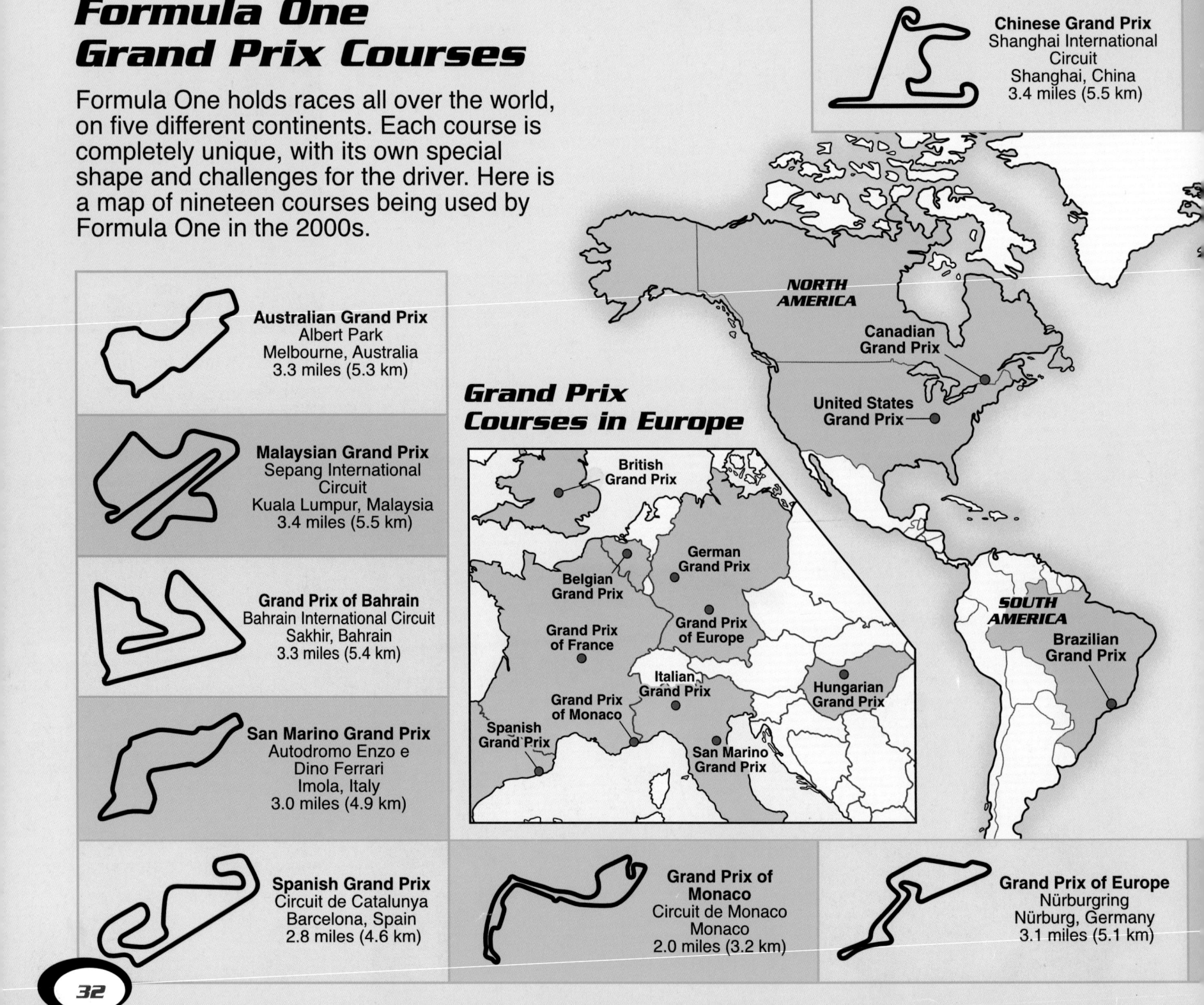

Chinese Grand Prix
Shanghai International Circuit
Shanghai, China
3.4 miles (5.5 km)

Australian Grand Prix
Albert Park
Melbourne, Australia
3.3 miles (5.3 km)

Malaysian Grand Prix
Sepang International Circuit
Kuala Lumpur, Malaysia
3.4 miles (5.5 km)

Grand Prix of Bahrain
Bahrain International Circuit
Sakhir, Bahrain
3.3 miles (5.4 km)

San Marino Grand Prix
Autodromo Enzo e Dino Ferrari
Imola, Italy
3.0 miles (4.9 km)

Spanish Grand Prix
Circuit de Catalunya
Barcelona, Spain
2.8 miles (4.6 km)

Grand Prix Courses in Europe

- British Grand Prix
- Belgian Grand Prix
- German Grand Prix
- Grand Prix of France
- Grand Prix of Europe
- Grand Prix of Monaco
- Italian Grand Prix
- Hungarian Grand Prix
- Spanish Grand Prix
- San Marino Grand Prix

NORTH AMERICA

Canadian Grand Prix

United States Grand Prix

SOUTH AMERICA

Brazilian Grand Prix

Grand Prix of Monaco
Circuit de Monaco
Monaco
2.0 miles (3.2 km)

Grand Prix of Europe
Nürburgring
Nürburg, Germany
3.1 miles (5.1 km)

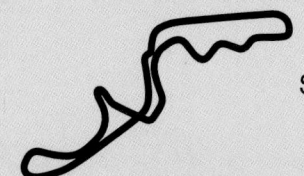

Japanese Grand Prix
Suzuka International
Race Course
Suzuka, Japan
3.6 miles (5.8 km)

Brazilian Grand Prix
Autodromo Carlos Pace
Sao Paulo, Brazil
2.7 miles (4.3 km)

Belgian Grand Prix
Circuit of Spa
Francorchamps
Francorchamps, Belgium
4.3 miles (7.0 km)

Italian Grand Prix
Autodromo Nazionale
di Monza
Monza, Italy
3.6 miles (5.8 km)

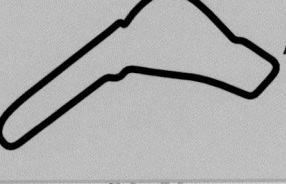

Turkish Grand Prix
Istanbul Park
Istanbul, Turkey
3.3 miles (5.3 km)

Hungarian Grand Prix
Hungaroring
Budapest, Hungary
2.7 miles (4.4 km)

German Grand Prix
Hochenheimring
Hochenheim, Germany
2.8 miles (4.6 km)

British Grand Prix
Silverstone Circuit
Silverstone, England
3.2 miles (5.1 km)

area of
inset
(facing page)

Turkish Grand Prix

ASIA

EUROPE

AFRICA

Chinese Grand Prix

Japanese Grand Prix

Grand Prix of Bahrain

Malaysian Grand Prix

AUSTRALIA

Australian Grand Prix

Canadian Grand Prix
Gilles Villeneuve Circuit
Montreal, Quebec
2.7 miles (4.4 km)

United States Grand Prix
Indianapolis Motor
Speedway
Indianapolis, Indiana
2.6 miles (4.2 km)

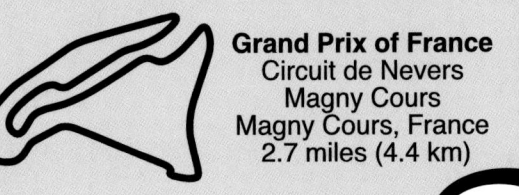

Grand Prix of France
Circuit de Nevers
Magny Cours
Magny Cours, France
2.7 miles (4.4 km)

FORMULA ONE GALLERY

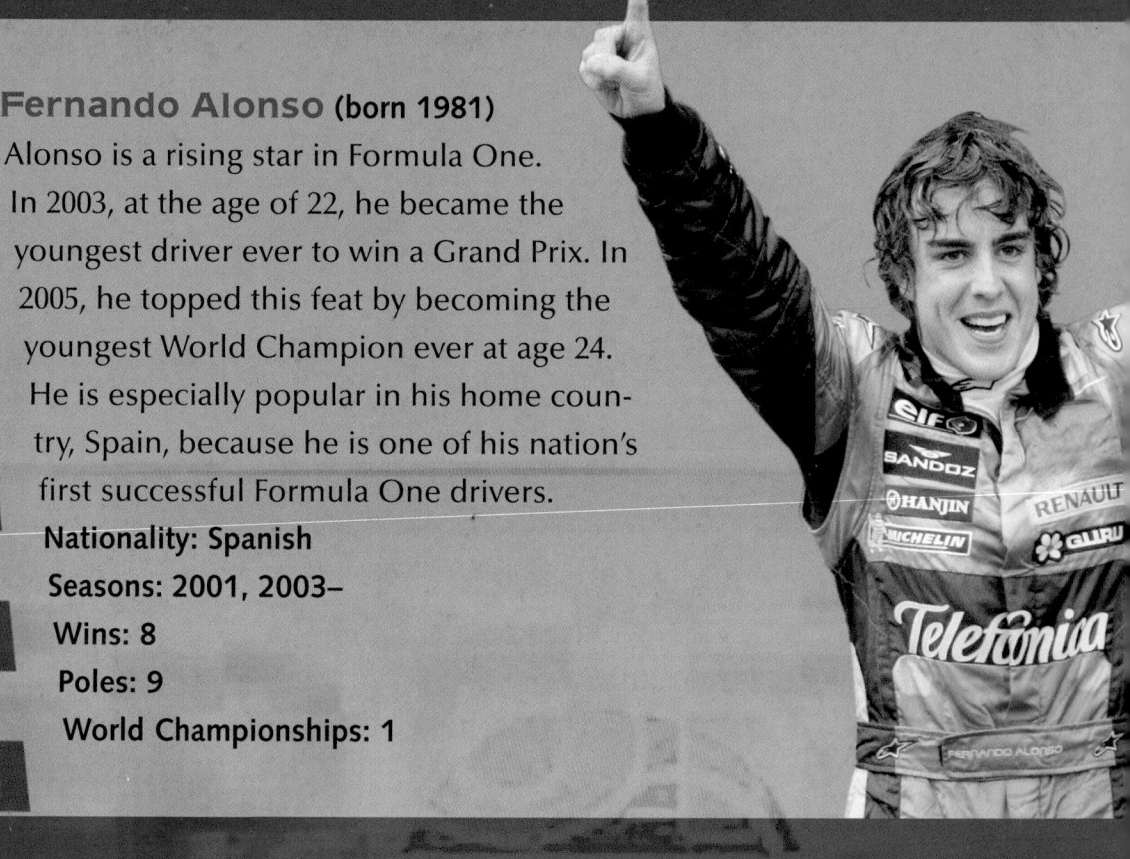

Fernando Alonso (born 1981)

Alonso is a rising star in Formula One. In 2003, at the age of 22, he became the youngest driver ever to win a Grand Prix. In 2005, he topped this feat by becoming the youngest World Champion ever at age 24. He is especially popular in his home country, Spain, because he is one of his nation's first successful Formula One drivers.

Nationality: Spanish
Seasons: 2001, 2003–
Wins: 8
Poles: 9
World Championships: 1

Mario Andretti (born 1940)

Born in Italy, this American is one of the great all-around drivers. He competed in Indy car races, NASCAR stock car races, and Formula One. In fact, he is the only person ever to win the Indy 500, the Daytona 500, and the Formula One World Championship.

Nationality: American
Seasons: 14 (1968–1972, 1974–1982)
Wins: 12
Poles: 18
World Championships: 1

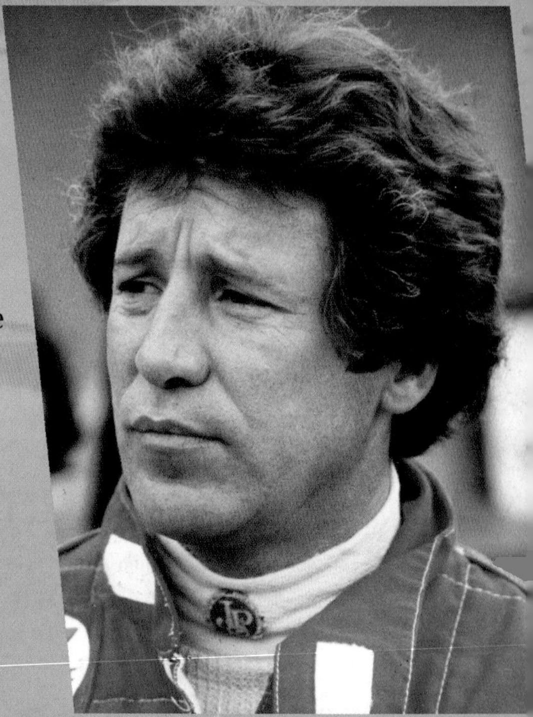

Fernando Alonso

Mario Andretti

Jack Brabham (born 1926)

This three-time World Champion was one of the first Formula One drivers to use a car with a rear engine. Brabham helped design his own cars and made important changes to the design and construction of Formula One cars.

Nationality: Australian

Seasons: 16 (1955–1970)

Wins: 14

Poles: 13

World Championships: 3

Jim Clark (1936–1968)

The talented Scot drove for the British Lotus team. The two-time World Champion also won the Indianapolis 500 in 1965. To the shock of the racing world, Clark was killed in a race in Germany in 1968.

Nationality: Scottish

Seasons: 9 (1960–1968)

Wins: 25

Poles: 32

World Championships: 2

Jack Brabham

Jim Clark

Juan Manuel Fangio (1911–1995)

Many consider Fangio to be the best racing driver ever. His record of five World Championships stood until Michael Schumacher snapped it in 2003. Fangio was known for his good sportsmanship, politeness, and personal charm.

Nationality: Argentine
Seasons: 8 (1950–1951, 1953–1958)
Wins: 24
Poles: 29
World Championships: 5

Mika Häkkinen (born 1968)

Häkkinen's Formula One career began in 1991. But he didn't score a win until 1997. From there, he became the circuit's top driver, winning the World Championship in 1998 and 1999. In 2000, Häkkinen lost the title to Schumacher after a number of mechanical failures knocked him out of important races. Häkkinen announced his retirement in 2002, but he continues to race in other series.

Nationality: Finnish
Seasons: 11 (1991–2001)
Wins: 14
Poles: 21
World Championships: 2

Juan Manuel Fangio

Mika Häkkinen

Stirling Moss (born 1929)

Moss is often called the best driver to never win a World Championship. He finished second overall in points four times. Passionate about racing, he also competed in sports car races. He retired from Formula One in 1962 after a nasty crash.

Nationality: British
Seasons: 11 (1951–1961)
Wins: 16
Poles: 16
World Championships: 0

Nelson Piquet (born 1952)

Known as a joker, the three-time World Champion was also a fierce competitor. His most famous rivalry was with British driver and Williams teammate Nigel Mansell. He retired after the 1991 season.

Nationality: Brazilian
Seasons: 13 (1979–1991)
Wins: 23
Poles: 24
World Championships: 3

Stirling Moss

Nelson Piquet

Alain Prost (born 1955)

Nicknamed "the Professor," Prost used smart strategies to win more races than anyone before him. He held the record for most wins until Michael Schumacher smashed it. McLaren teammate Ayrton Senna was his archrival, making for some exciting races in the late 1980s and early 1990s.

Nationality: French

Seasons: 13 (1980–1991, 1993)

Wins: 51

Poles: 32

World Championships: 4

Michael Schumacher (born 1969)

Schumacher has won more World Championships than any other driver. He broke Juan Manuel Fangio's record of five championships in 2003. He has also won the most races, making him statistically the best Formula One driver of all time. He is best known for driving for Ferrari.

Nationality: German

Seasons: 1991–

Wins: 84

Poles: 63

World Championships: 7

Alain Prost

Michael Schumacher

Ayrton Senna (1960–1994)

The beloved Brazilian driver was known for his incredibly fast driving and intensity. He won three World Championships before the age of 32. But his crash at the San Marino Grand Prix brought a tragic end to his life and great career.

Nationality: Brazilian

Seasons: 1984–

Wins: 41

Poles: 64

World Championships: 3

Jackie Stewart (born 1939)

Successful from the start of his Formula One career, Stewart won three World Championships. After he retired from racing, he worked to make Formula One safer for both drivers and teams. He has also worked as a sportscaster.

Nationality: Scottish

Seasons: 9 (1965–1973)

Wins: 27

Poles: 63

World Championships: 3